# ONE HEARTBEAT AWAY

### Author: Joe, The Poet

Compiled and Edited by: Michael Martin Scott

THIS PUBLICATION IS A WORK PRODUCT OF MAEJED, INC.
(MAEJED.COM)

# CONTENTS

## LOVE

## FREEDOM

# ABOUT THE AUTHOR

Joe, the Poet, was born to a single mother in February of 1976, and was the middle child of 8 sisters and 1 brother. Growing up in a large family gave Joe many life experiences from which to draw upon in his poetry compositions.

Joe, the Poet, grew up in St. Louis City, Missouri around the elements of poverty, gang violence and drugs. City life remains as challenging today as it was when Joe was born in 1976. Joe went to city public schools until dropping out in the 9th grade, when he decided to move in a different direction, needing more substance and inspiration in his life.

Joe, the Poet, never really attended regular church services growing up, although, his late grandmother did try to lead Joe and his family towards a semi-religious direction and background as Pentecostal Christians.

Joe, the Poet, loved spending his days listening to R&B love songs and hip hop music selections. From this, he first developed his talent and passion for expressing his thoughts and feelings with rhyme style, free verse, and prose. Joe created his own way of using the thoughts and emotions in his life and transforming them into words of bold expression. This, combined with Joe's later incarceration, ultimately created the foundation upon which he would later build to express his loves, heartbreaks, pains, prison emotions, and his curiosity of spiritual wisdom. These life experiences together led to the inspirations Joe needed to start writing his poetry and become "The Poet" that Joe truly is.

It is Joe, the Poet's, hope and prayer that his poetry not only express his take on life, but further helps to give others validation, inspiration, vision, and insight into their own thoughts and feelings, emotions and fears.

Joe's talent with rhyme style, free verse, and prose has the potential to reach us all.

~ Editor Michael Martin Scott

# DEDICATIONS

I sincerely dedicate my first book to my late brother, Alden Patrick Anderson (1980-2013); my friend and biggest fan. My brother wanted nothing but freedom and success for me.

My brother and I always tried to look beyond our downs and focused on making more ups between us.

To my brother: you may not be with me physically, but your presence will never die. No matter how far apart we are, you are only "One Heartbeat Away".

I miss you. I love you.


~ Joe, The Poet

# INTRODUCTION

"One Heartbeat Away" is a compilation of thoughts and emotions transformed into words. It is a mixture of different styles of poetry from free verse to prose.

Some poems are simply for humor like: "Once Upon A Time", which was written in an inspired five minute time period.

Some are more serious like: "The Storm", which was written during an emotional period at the beginning of my incarceration. "The Storm" was a product of my feeling like the walls were truly closing in on me.

There are poems for friends and family like: "A Birthday Star" written for my daughter, and "A Friend Indeed".

Love is indeed my favorite subject, and it shows with the many love poems offered in this book. It is surprising that the title poem "One Heartbeat Away" is one of the shortest, yet what I believe to be one of the most profound.

The title is universal and can express many of life's scenarios: one heartbeat away from love; one heartbeat away from freedom; or one heartbeat away from my family.

"One Heartbeat Away" sums up my feelings for most of my life's experiences and has helped me express myself in a productive way. Anyone with a love for poetry and free expression would love this book.

~ Joe, The Poet

## I Don't Know How

Sometimes I am just like a child, or a newborn baby,
Living and learning from scratch.
My mind wanders off and my thoughts get crazy,
And I know that it is Satan's attack.
I do not understand how I am getting knocked out,
When I am fighting with all of my strength.
Today I have faith in my heart with no doubt,
But tonight I will not know where it went.
I keep rushing in fast, and falling down hard,
Expecting a change right now.
Then I get discouraged and let down my guard,
Hoping God would help me somehow.
The things that are right; what I feel in my heart;
How I pray that I will carry them through.
But I don't know how, and it tears me apart.
I feel like I am not being true.
I am lacking the wisdom to focus my brain,
To keep Satan out of my head.
The thoughts in my mind bring me nothing but pain,
Yet I am seeking for pureness instead.
I need guidance, training, someone to teach me,
To pray and trust God as I should.
If my Father is in heaven, I need You to reach me,
And help me to live as You would.
I see Your example; I study Your Word,

## I Don't Know How

And I want to be patient for You.

But my flesh is forgetful of all that I have heard,

And the wonderful things You could do.

"Cast all of your cares, I will never forsake thee."

It seems God blinded my eyes.

Why would I want to carry my cross,

If he does not acknowledge my cries?

"Let the weak say they are strong; do not be afraid."

But I fear for my children each day.

Like Job, "my fears have come upon me."

I am not comforted, even when I pray.

"All things work for good, for them that love God."

And I will love Him and give Him my best.

I really cannot see any good around me.

But I have noticed this hole in my chest.

"I have good thoughts towards you" says God.

"A free and prosperous end."

Someone said, "We have a friend in Jesus."

If that is true, Lord, where is my friend?"

I hope to see clearly my life up the road,

And this pain is left miles behind.

With visions of lifting this old heavy load,

That no one can carry while blind.

I will continue to suffer, continue to struggle;

Continue to run this race.

I will continue to hold on to God through His Word,

'Till the day I see Him face to face.

## The Storm

I am going through a terrible storm;
While sitting patiently in a cell.
I try to focus my mind to Heaven,
But all I see is this living hell.
What is my life without my freedom?
Although I pray to free my mind.
I dream of family, Lord knows I need them.
God, just once rewind lost time!
I feel so much grief in my heart,
And my soul seems cut in two.
I imagine, daily, a brand new start.
Lord, help me cast my cares upon You.
With every good thought, tears form in my eyes;
I see visions of me – happy again.
I know that God has a Plan for my life,
And I have faith that this is not the end.
But what can I do when there is nowhere to go,
And no shoulders to support my lean?
When my freedom is life and prison is death,
And I am somewhere stuck in-between.
I will feel happy, then sad, content, then mad.
Lord, help the confusion all stop!
I will continue to ask and seek 'till I am blind,
And every door that is Yours I will knock.
I dread those days when I lay on my cot,
And time is slowly passing away quickly.

## The Storm

I will doze off to a dream and be with my family,

And love to have all of them with me.

Then I wake up to these concrete walls,

And I know that I am way out of place.

With my family at home, it is like I am unknown,

And I feel like I am such a disgrace.

I need strength when I am weak, I need wisdom to speak.

I need mercy to stop all my pain.

I need cool blowing wind with my children again;

To be under the sunshine and rain.

I need just one more chance, but until I see freedom,

I know that my heart will be torn.

God, change me, save me, do what You must,

To deliver me out of this storm.

## How Many Prayers?

How many prayers does it take,
To make my heart brand new?
To heal the hurt of my mistakes,
And the pain that I am going through?

How many prayers come from my heart?
How do I know when I am real?
Selfish emotions can tear me apart.
I could never trust how I feel.

How many prayers does it take,
To give me a pure righteous mind?
To help me choose the choices I make,
And show me where I have been blind?

How many prayers must it be,
To ease me of my heartache and blame?
All it takes is one prayer for me;
And that prayer is in Jesus' name.

## Overcoming Obstacles

They always make me lock down at night,
But they will never lock-up my mind.
This is not a place to get people right;
It is just a way to waste time.
The food they serve is garbage to me,
But I have the food that is not seen.
I am eating and growing spiritually,
All things that keep my soul clean.
My mattress is only two inches thin,
But still, I will sleep like a log.
They know I am a king deep within,
So they love treating me like a dog.
I am missing my friends and my family,
But I will be free once again.
This prison I am in cannot handle me,
'Cause God is my Father and friend.
They got me trapped inside of a cell,
But I still can see to the sky.
Trapped inside of this living hell,
But God will help me get by.
He sees this spiteful place I am in;
I know my blessings will come.
I refuse to let this obstacle win,
Because I am the victorious one.

## What I Have Been Missing

What I have been missing:

Is happiness; someone to brighten my day.

That sometimes acts wild, forces me to smile,

And chase all my sadness away.

What I have been missing:

Is companionship; a friend in my despair.

Soft, yet solid, and full of knowledge;

To know how to show that they care.

What I have been missing:

Is a gift; an elegant feminine present.

To share myself with, through thin and thick;

A love eternally pleasant.

What I have been missing:

Is opportunity; the time I did not know you.

Thank God for fate, it is not too late,

To lead us to something true.

What I have been missing:

Is you, Tiee; it seems I have a good chance,

To have time to spend with a lifelong friend,

And maybe even some romance.

## A Friend Indeed

To God I always beg and plead,
To send me a friend indeed.
A friend I trust with all I do.
A friend that is loyal, real and true;
A friend that understands my faults.
To have my back and have no doubts.
A friend to share my lifetime with,
To take my pain and carry it.
A friend to help me off the ground,
When my heart and soul is down.


A friend that loves to see me smile;
To laugh and joke with me a while;
To share our stories from the past,
And strive to make our friendship last.
A friend I know I can confide,
The hurts in life I hold inside.
A friend to let me ease their pain;
To reach for me when life is vain.
No longer will I beg and plead,
Because I have found my friend indeed.

## Togetherness

Once in a while someone comes along;
Physically fine, and mentally strong.
Someone who makes me feel happier;
You make me feel happier.


To make people feel more alive to life;
To bring out the feelings inside their life.
You have been that someone so dear to me;
To me it is clear to see.


Leslie, I am glad you are part of my life:
The music; the beauty; the art of my life.
It is truly a privilege to know you.
To share myself with you.


We will walk a path with clear directions.
With love divine, and honest affections.
Of all the chances we might have missed;
This, we shall not miss.


We were given a meant-to-be moment to meet.
Like winter's cold, or passion's heat;
To set the stage for togetherness.
To have a special togetherness.

## Thank You

Life can challenge us at times;

With so many ups and downs.

Troubles often stress our minds.

Between the smiles and frowns.

But there are times when those, like you,

Can pull me off the ground.

I thank you dear for all you do.

Helping turn my frown around.

## With Time

Happiness is seen in the heart, and in the mind,
And I am happy if you are happy,
With the growth I have made in time.

I have used these years to see my life,
And put it all in check.
All that is really on my mind,
Is gaining your respect.
The choices and mistakes I made,
Have made your life much rougher.
But I should have focused more on,
How not to make you suffer.
I lost a major part of my life;
What is a man to do?
But be true and apologize to you,
For what I put you through.
You did not deserve all,
The heartache, hurt, and pain.
I understand your feelings now,
I know I was the blame.
My mind is more secure,
And more mature in every way.
My priorities are not as dumb,
As way back in the day.
You were more than just the best for me,
But great for any man.

## With Time

God needed time to work on me;
I am sure you understand.
My idle mind was stuck back then;
Thought slow, but moved too fast.
Of course I feel remorse for how,
I treated you in the past.
Thanks for staying on my mind;
I know I left you alone.
Please look deep inside your heart,
Forgive me, I was wrong.
If you could only see me now,
You would be proud of me.
You would approve the sight you see;
The man I came to be.
Whether love was lost, or gained,
Let us walk on common ground.
I will reveal myself to you;
The new me that I have found.

Happiness is seen in the heart, and in the mind,
And I am happy if you are happy,
With the growth I have made in time.

## Don't Forget About Me

I have done some foolish things, and made some dumb mistakes,

But I am trying to change every day.

I have met many people, some real, some fake;

I have tried to help them anyway.

I am not always mad, but sometimes I am sad,

'Cause I would rather be happy and free.

It is those letters and pictures I surely wish I had,

But my family forgot about me.


They tell me they love me, so why am I lonely?

Showing me that they care would be nice.

Sometimes they act like they do not even know me,

But for years I have been part of their lives.

If they all needed me, I would help them with ease;

I believe that is how family should be.

If they only could see me, I would be on my knees,

Begging, "Please don't forget about me!"

## Happy Birthday – I Love You So Much

Your life has made my world like Heaven,
No doubt you came from above.
You are, will be, and always have been,
The one to show me true love.

My heart has turned to pure, solid gold;
You have stolen King Midas' touch.
God has blessed you to be another year old.
Happy Birthday, I love you so much.

## Birthday Star

I smile at you from afar,

'Cause in the sky there you are.

There you are,

A beautiful birthday star.

I gaze above night after night,

To look upon you shining so bright.

A twinkle little star I see;

The star that you are meant to be.

Inside my heart I love you so;

Outside I love to watch you glow.

I smile at you from afar,

'Cause in the sky there you are.

A beautiful birthday star,

Yes you are.

## Birth-Days

Birth is God's own special way;
Of loving all fathers and mothers.
Birth is why I thank God each day;
For you, your sisters, and brothers.


Days are light that shines on the heart;
And your days gave life to my soul.
Days were created to make light of dark;
And your days made my dark bright as gold.

## Mothers

Love is true love,

When expressed by a mother.

From newborns to infants,

Their love is like no other.

From infants to toddlers,

Our mothers were there,

To hold us and kiss us,

And show us they care.


From loving young toddlers,

To outrageous teens.

Our moms tolerate us,

Beyond any means.

From foolish teen years,

To so-called adults;

It is our mothers, who love us,

With all of our faults.


Thank you oh God, for my dear mother.

## My Life

My life is a joy,
But sometimes it is pain.
My life is like sunshine,
But sometimes it is rain.
My life is a life,
That I truly adore.
The love of my life,
Goes deep to my core.
And yes, it is beautiful;
This life that I know.
In my eyes, it is spotless,
Through rain, sleet, or snow.

If life is a dream,
Then I dream of it much.
The hearts it may feel,
And the hearts it may touch.
Some people live,
To make others smile.
Reaching out to their family,
Or raising a child.
There is no compare,
To my world and my life.
My world is my girl,
Any by life, I mean wife.

## Love Child

You are my heart, my life, and my world;

My love, strength, and sweet little girl.

I miss you more than words can say,

And I will hold you safely again someday.

I think of you often, daytime and night;

Laughing, playing, and hugging me tight.

I will always be honest, and true to you.

And I will have your back with all that you do.

My life will go on, I live for no other.

My love is for you, your sisters, and brother.

Be strong, do not ever forget about me.

You will see me again when I am happy and free.

## Once Upon A Time

I once had a dog named Red,
Who liked to sleep in my bed.
I kicked her out;
She started to pout,
So I put a slug in her head.

I once had a girl that was true,
Who pitied what I am going through.
Don't need that shit;
Hit her with a brick.
What else was a man to do?

I once had a friend named Bill,
Who claimed to always be real.
His friendship lacked;
I stabbed him in his back.
Now he knows how it feels.

I once was close to my kin,
Whether times were thick or thin.
Uncles, cousins, nieces;
I blew them all to pieces.
And now I sleep with a grin.

Do not tell me I am wrong.
Stop singing that old song.
Lost kids and a wife;
What a sorry life;
I guess I am where I belong.

## What's Right?

I am known as a victim from the present and past.
It was wrong how my offender made his shotgun blast.
He took aim and paralyzed me from my feet to my waist.
It is a shame when I am asleep I see his horrible face.
I blacked out and dark of night has taken over the day.
I heard a shout, but my offender managed to get away.
That is not right – do I have rights; why should I stay alive?
I see the light, I got to fight – I have the right to survive.
I am a victim when my sister was beat down and raped.
I am a victim when the one who shot my brother escaped.
I am a victim when that driver struck and killed my mother.
I am a victim when we do not show love for one another.
I have the right to stand strong and always speak my mind.
I have the right to stand against anyone doing crime.
I have the right to agree, or disagree, with a judge.
I have the right to forgive so I do not harbor a grudge.

## A Message To Hell

Dear God, would you please, send me a message to Hell.
To my father, we did not know each other so well.
He knows that I am jammed up, but tell him I am good.
Break it to him his ex-wife has passed, if you would.
Let him know there were questions I wanted to ask.
Like, was raising your first son really such a hard task?
And your sister that died when I was a baby;
Did she love me and hold me… yes, no, or maybe?
Why didn't you want me if you could not have mother?
She curses when she says how we look like each other.
I think of you often, but not every day.
Those thoughts were left empty when you drove away.
How could you just leave me when I was a kid?
Did you want to replace me, or was it something I did?
And what of my brother and sister you had?
Did you spend time with them, did they have a dad?

Dear God, please send me my message to Hell!
Ask Pop did he love me – I never could tell.
At times my mom would express to me madly,
"Get the hell out of my face; you act just like your daddy!!"
Should I not love my children since I act just like you?
I suppose you would tell me the right thing to do.
And God, ask Dad what is the meaning of life?
Should I roll, or be happy with kids and a wife?
Should I take advantage of those who are weak?
Should I lend an ear and let all people speak?
Should I create a legacy focused on greed?

## A Message To Hell

Should I open my heart; and give what I don't need?
Father, advise me on how I should live.
I need wisdom; perhaps you had wisdom to give.


Send my message to Hell, God; I am sure you know how.
Tell Dad I wish I could talk with him now.

## Imagine

Imagine someone so deep in your heart;
You picture their face with each beat.
And pray their love will never depart,
'Cause without them you would feel incomplete.


Imagine someone saying they love you,
And stopping your heart when they speak,
Someone honest, faithful, loyal, true,
And their beauty makes your knees get weak.


Imagine someone whom you share <u>one soul</u>;
<u>One Heart</u> and <u>one love</u> indiscreet.
Imagine grandchildren; grandparents grown old,
To live and to die so complete.

Seasons Love

### Winter's Night

The stars are clear.

The nights are cold.

I wish I were near,

For you to hold.

We will be forever,

As day has its light.

Staying warm together,

In the cold Winter's night.

### Spring Blossoms

Fresh love in the air,

For us to inhale,

Like your perfume and hair,

So sweet to the smell.

Flowers will grow,

And love birds will sing;

And our love is a rose,

That blossoms in Spring.

Seasons Love

## Summer's Love
A chance to love,
Shall not go undone;
Nor making love,
Under the sun.
Passion and heat,
Below skies above.
You and I are one,
Sharing Summer's love.

## Fall's Beauty
You are like a cool wind,
In the midst of the day.
A sunshine with no end,
Taking my breath away.
You are the one I adore,
And my love above all.
Our love shall grow more,
In the beauty of Fall.

## Angel Face

A world of delight in your eyes and smile;
This Earth revolves around you.
Planets worship your beauty and style;
My life isn't much without you.


The moon is amazed at the curve of your face;
So shapely and perfect in size.
The sun shows jealously, shame and disgrace;
'Cause there's more of a shine in your eyes.


Even flowers crave the breath of your air;
As fresh as a warm spring's breeze;
Your tears are as water to life everywhere;
Giving power to creatures and trees.


Angel, beautiful angel face;
Not only because you're my girl.
But all can see it from place to place;
And that is what you are to the world.

# Love

Have you ever felt someone so deep,
At times you could not eat or sleep,
Without them life seemed incomplete?
That's Love!

To think of someone all the time.
Right or wrong they are on your mind.
And to their faults your heart is blind.
That's Love!

At times when life is so unfair,
And no one seems to really care,
But someone loyal still is there.
That's Love!

Let us be real and never lie,
You will miss someone as time goes by;
Enough to make a grown man cry.
That's Love!

## A Time For Love

To everything there is a season,
And every heart should have a reason – To love.
There's a time to live and die,
And there's a time to laugh and cry – But love
There's a time to go away,
And there's a time that we must stay – To love.


A time for silence, and to speak;
A time to hide; a time to seek – For love.
There's a time to dance and sing,
And times we don't do anything – But love.
A time to win; a time to lose,
And times in life we have to choose – To love.


There's time to hurt, a time to heal;
And times to break so we can build – To love.
There's a time we should embrace,
And times we feel out of place – But love.
There's a time to let things go,
To find the time we need to grow – To love.

## All For You

I will give my life for you 99 times;

And I would, only if I could.

I would take all the bad days of your life,

And change them to make them all good.

I will go to Hell with no doubts in my mind,

And promise you that I will kill Satan.

I will destroy anything in this cold cruel world,

That causes my evil temptations.

For you, I would jump 'till I jump high enough,

Just to grab you the sun.

I would count endless stars without getting sleep,

Until YOU tell me I am done.

I would face 3 demons;

Slaughter tigers and bears.

For you I would fight anything, anywhere.

I would roam the desert for millions of days;

And still would find you in the world's biggest maze.

I would soar in the sky on top of a jet.

For you, I would dive straight off the top.

I would lay on all the train tracks in the world,

And make the Amtrak stop.

I would go to church 30 hours a day;

With Jesus Christ by my side.

I would bow down to you, and really be true,

And get rid of my foolish pride.

I would live on Mars, or under the sea;

With no air to help me breathe.

## All For You

I will survive off thoughts of you loving me,

'Cause your love is all that I need.

I would run around the globe, and swim every ocean;

For your love, I know that I can.

You should know – without a queen like you,

A man just isn't a man.

I would play tug-of-war with an 18-wheel truck,

And stop it dead in its tracks.

I would slap my own face 3-thousand times,

And dare me to smack myself back.

I would cherish and love you, hold you and hug you;

Adore you, and then love you much more.

I would take my time and do everything right,

And live life like I should have before.

I would always be joyful, and never act mean,

And respect all your family and friends.

I would do anything, and I mean ANYTHING!!

To have you in my life 'till the end.


As long as you are in my Heaven;

I know that I am never going to burn.

## Beauty Queen

There is the warmth of the sun within your eyes;
The smile of the moon, where your heart lies.
Maybe my God did not realize,
He blessed you with all of that beauty.


Your precious face; you should never disguise;
Your beauty causes my heart rate to rise.
Time after time, I just fantasize,
And thank God for all of your beauty.


I declare you the best, like you are royalty.
I honor your love, and your loyalty;
And crown you as queen, for all to see;
Because to me you are the queen.


I will bow to your feet, if you ask of me.
Be guard over you, as a man should be.
Pledge undying love, as deep as the sea,
'Cause you are my beauty queen.

## Dream

I dreamt a dream that somebody loved me;
A love that needs no explanation.
In my dream she seems to never ignore me;
And love me with no hesitation.


The dream I dreamed was only for me,
And real as this heart in my chest.
Adoring my dream, in my eyes I see,
A love that's unlike all the rest.


My world is a dream when I am awake.
The love from my dream is still present.
A dream worry free of hearts that break;
Just warm, strong, loving, and pleasant.

## Heart and Soul

Love comes from above;
Goes deep as the soul.
And finding true love,
Is man's ultimate goal.
You are set like a seal,
Upon my brave heart.
Our love is like steel,
Even though we're apart.
My strength came from pain;
My courage from aches.
You keep my mind sane,
With whatever it takes.

Independent, yet nice;
So beautiful, yet strong.
The star in my life,
Where, Lord knows, you belong.
We have that connection;
That bond and that care.
That love and affection,
Forever we'll share.
You gave me your heart;
Your help and your time.
You'll always be part,
Of this soul of mine.

## Lovely Orchids

Flowers create many loving sensations,
From daisies to lilies, and even carnations.
Picture us staring out over the hills,
Or lying out stretched on plush daffodils.
Inhaling the jasmine while we cuddle so tight,
And sharing a kiss as we say goodnight.


The flower for you would not be a rose.
But a tropical, lovely orchid I suppose.
With radiant petals that are warm and bright.
Like your smile, a beautiful treat for my sight.
The love that we share would never depart.
You're my flower, my orchid, and queen of my heart.

## My Distant Valentine

My distant valentine, so close to my heart.
Far away, yet in me so deep.
No one on Earth could keep us apart,
And my love is all yours to keep.

I will lift your soul, as you hold me down;
'Cause the love in my heart cannot hide.
It does not matter what state, city, or town;
I trust you will be by my side.

To love through hard times is true love indeed.
In storms our love life will stand.
Oh Tina, you know that you got what I need,
So believe, trust, and wait on your man.

You are the sweetest heart, and my far away lover;
In due time our passions will start.
Thank God he gave me a heart to discover,
My distant valentine so close to my heart.

## I Love You Because

I love you because,

You are my light when it is dark,

Like the sun that brightens my day.


I love you because,

You bring life to my heart;

A goddess in your own special way.


I love you because,

I am fulfilled;

My love is overflowing for you.


I love you because,

My spirit gets thrilled,

When you show that you love me too.

As the sky and the doves;

We should be together,

You and I, so joyous and free.


I love you because,

My love is forever,

Because I know that you love me completely.

## My Everything

You are my light in the darkness;
My day after night.
Whenever I am wrong,
I have you to be right.

You are my up when I am down;
When I am low you are my high.
You are my breath of fresh air,
When the wind pass me by.

You are the wishes I make;
All my dreams when I sleep.
You are my prayers to God,
And my strength when I am weak.

You are my smile when I am sad;
My life, world and Earth.
You are my heart doctor,
Whenever it hurts.

You are a treat for my eyes,
And you look very nice.
You are the homie and friend,
That I want as my wife.

When I feel down and out,
You are a shoulder to lean.
In my heart, soul and mind,
You are my everything.

# Anniversary

The day my life has its greatest value.
A day designed to bring us close.
From past to present, and all that I will do;
I do for the one I love most.


Anniversary;
A day to reflect my biggest victory;
Victorious in winning your heart.
A day celebrated throughout all of history;
A day that would top any chart.


Anniversary;
A day when God looks down and smiles;
When the sun is as bright as your soul.
The day love peaks with poetic style;
Assuring our hearts will not grow cold.

## My Head In The Sky

Every day I know I am living to die,

But this girl has got my head in the sky.

I start believin'that I really could fly;

'Cause this girl has got my head in the sky.


High as a kite, she sweeps me off my feet;

Hearing her voice, to me, is always a treat.

When life is over I will be on cloud nine,

Because this girl has control of my mind.

I want her in my life until I depart;

Heaven help me show her my true heart.


Every day I know I am living to die,

But this girl has got my head in the sky.

I start believin'that I really could fly;

'Cause this girl has got my head in the sky.


God's angel got me floating around;

I never, ever, want to touch back down.

She lifts my spirits with the words she would say;

She keeps my soul rising day after day.

It is not so bad leaving out of this world;

Knowing that I have a heavenly girl.


It does not matter knowing that I will die;

'Cause this girl has got my head in the sky.

## My Only Desire

Nothing worth having is easy to hold,
But I have you inside of my heart.
Sometimes love hurts, or so I am told;
And without you I would fall apart.
No urges, no lusts, no wants, no needs.
My satisfied heart is on fire
No more envy, or dying of greed.
In this world you are my only desire.

I have wanted all things from diamonds to gold;
The cars, the clothes, and the girls.
I have even wanted to never grow old,
And somehow take charge of the world.
With all foolish things that I have possessed;
I refuse to let life expire;
Without ever saying that you are the best;
My love, and my only desire.

Nothing compares to the feeling you bring.
No one can match all you do.
You are like a drug that makes my heart sing,
And I love being addicted to you.
You are all that I need for the rest of my days;
All I want 'till my soul retires.
I wish I could say it in one million ways;
You are my first, and my only desire.

You are my first thought in the morning,
And my only desire at night.

## My Thoughts Of You

Believe I love you, because I do.
Believe I want you, because I do.
Believe you complete me, because you do.
Believe my world revolves around you.


I need you to believe I will die for you.
Not because I tell you, but because it is true.
I need you to tell me what to do.
Because all of my thoughts are of you.

## One Love

One love like the woman who gave me life;
One love like a hug from the sky.
One love like a child by a beautiful wife;
One love like fresh air passing by.


One love like a mind that is always free;
One love like forbidden love pleasures.
One love like a soul that has love for me;
One love is worth more than all treasures.

## Only Gods Knows

Only God knows,
What I feel in my heart.
In my eyes it shows;
In this soul it starts.

Only God can see,
How deeply I love you;
Much deeper than seas,
The rivers run to.

Lord knows deep inside,
Our love will not die;
As high love birds glide;
So strong are you and I.

God knows that I hurt,
Whenever you are stressed.
He keeps me alert,
When you are sad and depressed.

My God is aware,
Of our trials and tasks.
My love is always there;
You do not need to ask.

Only God knows,
When my heart is real.
Lord knows you are a rose,
Alone in a field.

## Picture Perfect

A picture is worth a thousand words.
And yes, I believe that is true.
It seems unreal what my heart heard,
When I laid my eyes upon you.

Tina, what is it that makes you smile?
And why are your eyes so bright?
I am sure they shine for miles and miles,
Like the moon that brightens the night.

Tina, how can I learn your ways?
You seem to be smart and sincere.
How do you handle your good and bad days?
And what do you hold close and dear?

Tina, your picture is a photo with love.
Isn't that what I see in your eyes?
Of course you're an angel from Heaven above;
A sweet, sexy, chocolate surprise.

Tina means loving, caring and peaceful,
Honest, pure, loyal and true.
Not evil, nor rude, and never deceitful.
My pleasure would be loving you.

## Smile I Ask

Smile I ask – smile for me;
Smile when the world causes pain.
Smile when life is as low as can be;
In sunshine, and even through rain.
Smile like a 10 million lottery winner.
Smile brighter than nights filled with stars.
Smile like "new life" to a born again sinner,
Redeemed and healed from all scars.

Smile I ask – smile for me.
Smile like there's no care at all.
Smile like that day God gave you me;
My wedding, but your princess ball.
Smile like you smiled when you turned 21;
We partied and had lots of fun.
Smile for our boy when I shed tears of joy;
When you said you were having my son.

Smile, my dear; smile for me.
Think of a reason to smile.
Just try, and if you can't, smile for me.
I know there is something worthwhile.

## The Greatest Sensation

You are all the things that would please any man.
From your kiss all the way to the touch of your hand.
Your sweet sounding voice that keeps my head spinning.
Your eyes captured me from the very beginning.
Lusting for you is the greatest temptation,
But having your love is the greatest sensation.

Your vibe is a warm and tingly feeling.
The best when it comes to a sexual healing.
My eyes are in awe of your extreme beauty.
My body cannot handle the things you do to me.
I get joy and hope from your conversation,
But your love for me is the greatest sensation.

Your smile sends me signals my mind never knew;
And my heart's telling me that it loves to love you.
My soul is amazed 'cause you are in it so deep,
And my arms want to hold you, to have you to keep.
I have no doubt you are God's greatest creation,
And your love for me is the greatest sensation.

## You Chose Me

When life was young, and options plentiful,
And Mama's boy had nothing to offer –
You chose me.


You chose me to be the love of your life –
To have a son and raise him right.
Discouraged by friends and family – yet,
You still chose me.


You chose me to chase your pain away.
Against all the odds this cruel world creates –
You had to see something in my heart,
Because you chose me.

## If You Don't Mind

If you don't mind;
I would smother you with passions unknown,
And reveal how true love should be shown.
I would appreciate the time that we share,
And do anything to prove that I care;
If you don't mind.

If you don't mind;
I would give my all 'cause you deserve the best;
And pay all the bills, so you don't have to stress.
My first priority is taking care of you,
And do all the things a man in love should do;
If you don't mind.

If you don't mind;
I would keep you safe and spoil you like a child.
Buy you nice things just to see you smile.
All would know; I am your man, you are my girl;
That would not change for anything in the world;
If you don't mind;
If you don't mind.

## A Dream Come True

With few pictures in sight of your beauty to see;
I still have all my dreams to entertain me.
Dreams of your face, and the way that you smile;
Dreams of your touch that drives me so wild.
Laughing and playing with kisses and hugs;
Any dream of you is a dream filled with love.


I dream of us eating and sleeping together.
I dream of you saying you will love me forever.
I dream of us dancing to our favorite song;
I dream of how sexy you have looked all along.
I dream you are an angel from Heaven above.
I now realize that you are all I dream of.


You are truly a dream come true.

# Each Day

Each day my love for Tina grows and grows,
And where it will stop nobody knows.
Her eyes are so bright and beautiful to see;
And my heart skips a beat when she looks at me.
I sometimes get speechless, or lose words to say;
And I wish I could have her more each day.
To touch her and hold her, to kiss and to hug;
To adore and caress her, and to give her my love.


Each day my love for Tina grows and grows,
And where it will stop nobody knows.
Enticing and tempting, so nice and so sweet.
She has all the right curves from her head to her feet.
Her waistline and stomach, those cheeks and those lips;
Her neck and her back, those thighs and those hips.
I want her and need her, it is hell being apart.
Right now I cannot have her, but she has my heart.


Each day my love for Tina grows and grows...

## Cruel Nights and Hurtful Days

Cruel nights and hurtful days;
My heart is doomed without you.
Tear filled eyes with a lifeless gaze;
My soul will not live without you.

Painful sobs and throbbing aches;
My spirit cries without you.
This unkind heart gives me no breaks;
Love does not love me without you.

Insane, sad and blue desire;
My life is void without you.
"She misses me". My heart is a liar;
I know no truths without you.

Like a seed, dirt covers me;
Good thoughts do not sprout without you.
I am like a snail beneath a tree;
Sunny days are cursed without you.

Soft winds blow my strength away;
I am weak and broke without you.
Each night is cruel; I hurt each day.
My heart is damned without you.

## One Heartbeat Away

I am one heartbeat away from loving again;
It is coming like clouds and rain.
I once knew love as a foe, not a friend,
And with every heartbeat I felt pain.


Even though I lost love, I am willing to try,
To receive it, and conquer my fear.
Love has the strength to make grown men cry;
With each heartbeat there is heartache and tears.

## Lost And Found

Where does love go when no one is there?
My heart was longing for someone to care.
With every beat, I fell further away,
Still hoping for love, day after day.
I misplaced love, and searched all around;
What once was lost, thank God I found.


My days were dark, no love in my sight;
I reached for my love night after night.
Then love returned, to my surprise;
She came as an angel with beautiful eyes.
Now my heart feels more safe and sound;
For, my love was lost, but now she is found.

## Never Fall Again

I swear to never fall again;
I will not slip any more.
I always want to have a friend,
But love has closed its doors.

If I shall fall, I shall break;
The pain would hurt so bad.
My loving heart was a mistake;
The heart that I once had.

I vow to never love again;
As silly as it sounds.
I will not lie, nor pretend,
But always stand my ground.

If love approaches face to face;
I am ready for a fight.
If I fall I'll flee the place,
And run with all my might.

I promise not to fall again;
I tell myself each day.
Love is a game I cannot win,
Nor bear the price to pay.

The hurt just seems to never end;
Believe my words are true.
I pray I never fall again,
UNLESS I fall for <u>you</u>.

## She Loves Me Not

She loved me, yes, with all her heart,
Like a rose that loves the sun.
Our fiery love has lost its spark,
And a love was left undone.

She missed me, yes, with all her mind.
Like dry ground misses the rain.
All thoughts of love have been unkind,
Love has no pleasure, just pain.

She loved me, yes, this once was true,
Like two people sharing one soul.
Her heart has turned from red to blue,
And her heated love grew cold.

Memories of love are all I've got,
How I wish that love was still strong.
She loved me, now she loves me not,
But my life will still go on.

## 'Till Death Do Us Part

### ( A Die Hard Love)

There has been a death, but not of flesh and blood;
The death of my feelings, emotions, and love;
The death of the plans that I made for my life;
The death of intentions on keeping a wife.
I am dying to feelings I felt in my heart;
And recall myself vowing, "'Till death do us part."

To die hard means – determined to put up a fight;
To hold on to lost love with all of your might.
Dying hard is – resisting the odds that are hopeless;
To hold firmly to someone that won't even notice.
I died hard to a love that was left in my heart.
When loves dies, it is a death that has done us apart.

I will show no affection; my heart can't be led;
The love I once had in my heart is now dead.
Apart from each other, we lost our true love;
A love that once was from Heaven above.
A die hard love is now dead in my heart;
And I meant it when I vowed, "'Till death do us part".

## Right Mind

Strange is the look,
On my face in this place.
Pain is what I feel,
Mixed with hurt and disgrace.

Lame would describe,
The life I now live.
Blame is to me,
For myself to give.

Shame is the feeling,
While living alone.
Strained is my brain,
So far from my home.

Dark is my past;
And I hate to remember.
My freedom attacked,
Like the World Trade Center.

A part of my pain,
Is just all in my head.
I will start going insane,
If they leave me for dead.

A spark starts a flame,
That ignites in my mind.
To scorch the poor heart,
That has left me behind.

## Sounds of a Cell

Sounds surround me in my seclusion;
These sounds just will not let me go.
The sounds of grief, mistakes and confusion,
Locked down with nowhere to go.

Listen, the walls blowing air like whirlwinds;
Destroying what heat I might feel.
I hear men praying for family and friends,
Giving God all their evils to heal.

I hear sounds of convicts yelling and cussing;
Preparing for their biggest fight.
The sounds of cellies arguing, fussing,
And blowing hot air half the night.

I hear sounds of a toilet's vicious roar;
Like a lion that is caught in a snare.
Above I hear batteries tap dancing the floor,
And someone playing slide with a chair.

I hear dominoes making the sound of keys,
So I check for a guard in my view.
I hear fools on the phones chanting, "Please baby please"!
As 'tho they still don't have a clue.

But the most discrete sound I perceive,
Is a voice that I hear in my slumber.
A soul; a spirit, pleading to leave;
An essence that jail took under.

## If I Get Free

If I get free;
I will show my loved ones I love 'em.
Never act like I am above 'em;
Pull them close to me and hug 'em.
If I get free,
It is going to be a celebration;
How I conquered my temptation,
To control my situation.
If I get free,
I will put the past far behind;
Clear the evil out of my mind,
And look ahead for better times.
If I get free,
I will only focus on what is right;
Live day by day, and not by the night,
And walk by faith into the light.
If I get free,
I will choose the people I am around;
Never let them bring me down;
To keep my feet on solid ground.
If I get free,
I will let the public see me grow;
Appreciate the ones I know;
Enjoy my life and take it slow.
Lord knows;
If I get free.

## I Am Not Alive

At night I pray to God, and I know that I'm forgiven.

I have breath in my lungs, but still, this is not livin'.

I feel my chest beating; I know that I have a heart,

But being locked in this prison is tearing it all apart.


Sometimes I feel unwanted, stressed out and confused.

Sometimes it is hard to follow all these man made rules.

Each morning my eyes open, but still I am dying slowly.

My life has turned around, now I do not even know me.


Who is that in the mirror where I see my reflection?

I do not like being in jail; who made that selection?

Exactly what was I thinking when I was out doing wrong?

Why did it never occur to me that I will be all alone?


I feel like it is all a dream; I eagerly try to wake.

Does not God have compassion for people who makes mistakes?

These are hard times; I guess my heart should be hard-core,

And I will be losing my mind until I am out of this door.


I am not alive; I am trapped far away from my home.

I am not alive – fighting not to do what is wrong.

I am not alive; I never thought it would come to this.

I am not alive, homeboy; I only exist!


God should never have made me; why did He create me?

I do not understand why I survived as a baby.

I should have been long gone; no knowledge of war and peace.

Is this why I am full grown; to watch all my troubles increase?

## I Am Not Alive

I don't get it; I ain't with it; in the hands of the wicked.
Who can split Heaven and Hell on a one-way ticket?
All this terror hurt and pain; I know I can survive,
But would rather see the streets – working 9 to 5;

Staying alive, enjoying freedom at full-force.
With friends and family having fun – and money of course.
Take all that away and I'm simply just a dead man.
Ain't no better days; got to get that through my thick head man!

But let us not talk about it; my life, forget about it!
Everyone can live without it; miss me? I really doubt it.
Out of sight means out of mind when you are trapped in a net.
Got so many regrets, do not know what is next, 'cause…

I am not alive; I am trapped far away from my home.
I am not alive – fighting not to do what is wrong.
I am not alive; I never thought it would come to this.
I am not alive, homeboy; I only exist!

I write insane words because of a broken heart.
It seems my life ended before it could ever start.
Do not know if I have a soul; do not feel like I have a spirit;
And death is nothing new, that is why I will never fear it.

But I am suffocating, and only want a chance to breathe.
It is frustrating waiting for my chance to leave.
And nerve racking; every night I am begging God please.
Give me a second to show you I can raise my seeds!

## I Am Not Alive

But I am helpless; this ain't the way I envisioned my life;
By doing wrong – knowing that I should have done right.
My existence is a tragedy, many people are mad at me.
Satan is here to hassle me, just to make me a casualty.

Hold up! Let us stop before this gets any worse.
I am a son of God; why is it that I am living a curse?!
How bad does it get? I know it is not the end of my battles yet.
I am all upset; knowing I exist, but I will never forget…

I am not alive, homeboy; I only exist!!!

## I Still Exist

I spend time in a cage, but I still exist;
My mind is constantly growing.
I refuse to let rage, backed up by my fist,
Hinder all wisdom worth knowing.

My faith is in God, my trust is in time,
'Cause for sure it will keep passing by.
It should not seem odd, nor confuse the mind,
That in due time we all must die.

My loved ones are distant, but I still exist.
The life I once lived is no more.
My family refuses to deal with this mess,
But I lifted my will off the floor.

Grown men should be strong, and ready to die;
Concrete and steel to the core.
Correct me if I'm wrong, 'tho we don't cry;
We've all shed our tears once before.

Go examine yourselves, as tough as you are,
And tell me, what do you see?
Is it diamonds and wealth, rims on a car;
Or just a man that wants to be free?

Some people reject me, but I still exist;
So long as I guard my own health.
Hate, but respect me, and always know this;
This man can think for himself.

## I Still Exist

"Pray", they say, "Speak as we speak".
Stand back – let me use my own brain.
Day after day I get strength if I'm weak;
Only God can conquer my pain.

We know this is not living, but we still exist;
We all have this one common link.
If one thing is worth giving to those we miss;
It is showing we have learned how to think.

Take pride in our thoughts, stay focused and clear;
Impressing ourselves every day.
Forgive our own faults, overcome our fears,
And rest in good peace as we lay.

Encourage our families, by phone, or by mail;
Especially the young and the free.
Teach them priorities, and if all else fails,
For a bad example, use me.

Whatever it takes; whatever you need;
Stress the fact that they do not want this.
We made the mistakes, let us hope they take heed;
This is not living, but we still exist.

From prison walls.

## No Evil

Should I hear no evil...

    When the judge says, "Life",

    And that gavel makes the sound

    Of chains shackling slaves

    As it strikes the wood?

Should I hear no evil...

    When someone says, "Die you die"!!

    Not to my face,

    But to my heart?

Should I see no evil...

    When the eyes of those imprisoned,

    In body, mind, or soul,

    Show the agony that life

    Has relentlessly poured upon them?

Should I see no evil...

    When I witness the savage

    Face of racism that refuses

    To vanish and wither away?

## No Evil

Should I speak no evil…

    When those, like me,

    Spit burning words of fire,

    And scorch the little

    Peace I may have left?

Should I speak no evil…

    When I am asked

    What I did wrong, I reply,

    "What did you do wrong:?


Ask me question – I tell no lies.

Better yet, don't ask me SH--!!

FREEDOM

## Living In A Cemetery

Livin' in a cemetery, with gravestones and bodies buried;
Tryin' to find a place to hide from all my worries.
It is kind of scary how this became my home.

Tell my enemies it is on;
Shot my homie, now he is dead and gone.
I paid a visit to the burial site, angry with all my might;
Drinkin' Hennessey had me there all night.

I've never been the type to say I'm really spiritual;
To go back home now, is gonna take a miracle.
I keep my .45 by my side at all times;
Reflecting my crimes, to the police, I am hard to find.

Show me a sign of life I'm supposed to lead.
Is it weed, or greed, or simply just to take care of my seed?
My life ain't complete, destiny is hard to beat;
Night after night, I find myself always fallin' asleep.

Let the truth be known – that life does go on.
No pillows to fluff; got me sleepin' on a gravestone.
I am chillin' like a villain, lonely is how I am feelin';
But ready and willin' for killin' – cemetery livin'…

## Living In A Cemetery

Through rain, sleet or snow, tonight is just another night;
Talkin' to my dead homie, I got the feelin' something aint' right.
I get hyped, and all I'm thinking is to blow some stuff up;
All my so-called homies, never seem to show up!

My mind clicked, got me feelin' like a lunatic;
With all this darkness 'round me, I'm 'bout to have a fit.
No money, no cars, not girls 'round me to lie to;
I read the Bible to keep from feelin' suicidal.

Who am I to neglect the ones that got love for me;
I'm high as can be – how is it that I'm drug free?
Sleepless night is a sight to see when it is judgment day;
To see the sight of so-called family, so quick to turn away.

When will I smile again – what the hell is going on?
Where is this life takin' me?
Why can't I find my way back home?

Two in the morning, wakin' up screamin', "Lord hurry!"
But startin' to worry – livin' in a cemetery…

FREEDOM
## Living In A Cemetery

Now understand…


I'm getting visits from moms, my kids and my wife;

And that's nice, but it's like I live a double life.

All that time I tried to reach out and get a hug;

All that time I seen my kids with a mean mug.


Missing signs – can't even kiss my wife and tell her bye.

Momma act blind, talkin' to me but lookin' at the sky;

Askin' why – don't nobody cry, just leave it alone.

I think somethin' went wrong; a true man gonna stay strong.

That thug livin' got the best of me.

Too many was busy testin' me; as a result, I'm restin' in peace.


Even my .45 left me alone;

Now that it's gone, I can do no wrong where I call home.

It is a pity;

Feelin' not quite so witty.

No more postin' up shop;

Anxious to pull out my Glock.

Instead, I'm layin' countin' the raindrops;

As I sleep in the same spot wondering when will the pain stop.


No questions asked; I cannot handle the truth.

When they blasted my homie; they blasted me too.

Graveyard dreams got me 'visioning myself buried;

But feelin' no worries and livin' in a cemetery.

## Testing, Testing

Testing, testing, is this thing on?
Can somebody tell me where we went wrong?
Grabbing this weapon; going on that mission;
What happened to goals, aspirations, ambition?

There is jealousy and plotting on so-called friends;
When envy starts, compassion ends.
Stagnated by hate, going nowhere fast;
Our present and future have to do with our past.

Ropes, whips, crosses burning;
Some people still think we are incapable of learning.
"This is a new era, those days are long gone";
But there will always be haters we need to prove wrong.

"I have to prove nothing", I am hearing you fool;
Being broke, dumb and locked up will never be cool!
There's bitterness, depression, a lack of affection;
The human race needs more lessons – any suggestions?

Who could answer the question, "What's the meaning of life?";
To show what love is, or war, murder and strife.
This life isn't nice for the cowardly weak;
Scared to hold their heads high and express their belief.

## Testing, Testing

Each man has a purpose – that is what I believe;
Some to inspire, and some to deceive.
To uplift, motivate, to rebuild and heal;
To crush people's dreams, and find hopes to steal.

Charity, honesty, doing God's will;
Lying, or hunting for someone to kill.
Teaching, encouraging to invent the next wheel;
It all plays a part in the hand that life deals.

That's real – each man has a story to tell;
Let's learn from the past and move forward from Hell

Testing, testing, is this thing on??

www.ingramcontent.com/pod-product-compliance
Lightning Source LLC
Chambersburg PA
CBHW081438090426
42740CB00017B/3353